WHERE THE FENCELINE RUNS

DAVE BARBER

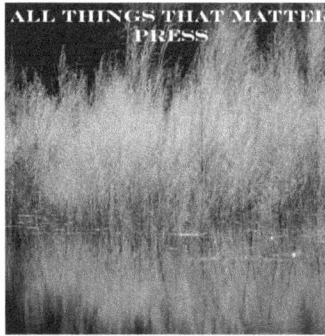

WHERE THE FENCELINE RUNS

ISBN: 0-9822056-4-3

ISBN 978-0-9822056-4-8

LIBRARY OF CONGRESS NUMBER: 2008941211

PHOTOGRAPHS BY HELEN BARBER

COVER DESIGN BY ALL THINGS THAT MATTER PRESS

PUBLISHED IN 2008 BY ALL THINGS THAT MATTER PRESS

PRINTED IN THE UNITED STATES OF AMERICA

DEDICATION

This book is dedicated to my sweet, sweet wife
who puts up with my non-sense and loves me
through every up and down.

Thank you!

Table of Contents

TASTES

My daughter loves red licorice;
she twirls it around her fingers
in rings and necklaces dreaming
of sweet new days.

I wish she'd grow up.

My daughter loves to mix sodas
into strange concoctions she
drinks and smiles, burping
around her friends.

I sigh at the thoughts.

She aims her camera in quick snaps
laughing as she shakes the picture
and tries to frames it perfectly, her
calendar covered with her friend's drawings

She's shy around those, she doesn't know,
but waltzes around in slow happy circles
smiling at her stuffed animals.

Why predict her growth, in terms
of silly matters at home.
Now she doesn't like licorice.
She grew too fast.
(11 Jan 06)

WHY THESE?

I've been thinking of lilies
As they arise like pillars of spring
In the garden,
Pillars of life?

But why are they thought of
In the passing of a human
Into the evening
Not a bringing of life?

As an old idea
If I was a lily,
Would I bring smiles
Of the bees who visit?

Forgetting myself
Even in the feathery fields
Bright and calming
In the face of snow.

Wondering through fields
Where the lily fades
Without a protest
Just rises and floats away.

10 April 05

SOCIAL

My wife is angry
And I wonder what she'll do
But she holds herself quiet
Like the willow still air
And sips the conversation
In tiny gulps.
(It's all she can take.)
Comments about her work
And music will come
O yes! They will
And what will they think?
Take another cup
Bitter sweet,
Shall we drink
And not see the cup?
(I shall hear it later)
I know the trouble is there
And my heart flutters.
I feel her heart go wild
As the blanket flowers
Weaved in colors outside
Hiding the deep trouble.
Here we are again,
Tending our social duties.

9 July 05

UNTITLED

I shared my father's love for the night skies
He'd peer up into the night and name each
Star, as if they'd grown up next to him
In that shabby, fallen, shot-gun house
The one with the white flaking paint-

Flaking into the sky
Yes, that's Orion, hanging high and bright
After the sun completed her performance
Mauve skies had faded to black
A shining crescent moon, cupped around a dark friend.

My shadow cast its patina over the night. My father's
Graying, thinning hair somehow shining in the night too
His face tilted to the sky, like a plant reaching for light.

I wondered if he needed the light of stars to dream
Or flower, to seed himself a thousand times was we slept.

To the north, the lights of downtown city shone. My Dad
Wishing they'd fade, then going back to pointing. The
stars seemed jumbled into a strange mass but ordered.
And I was out of place in in that order- they reminded
me. Growing up in Texas, My father told me where I stood

In relation to stars, life. I was far below the Big
Dipper and light-years from Alpha Centaur, But I could always
orient myself - fix myself on the North Star.

If I could find that,
I could find my way
Never get lost. No matter what.

HOW MANY SURFACES?

Now the drop has become one,
World's larger -
Reflecting the surface only
A greater freedom in the new
Union or just the same.

Reflections are backwards
My face in the drop
Is upside down
Distorted and stretched
Into a new place

Self sees the day
Ended in evaporation
Surface is gone - for now
Dried into the next time
I'm wondering about the next time.

1 Jan 05

BORN

Death did not come like a friend
It would be birthed
Like others things brought
Through waters.

Chasing my mother across the bed
Yelling, help me!
But death was slow
And it waited.

When it was born,
We took and covered him-
Wrapped him up carefully,
Sat him beside her.

So they could both rest.

13 Dec 04

CYCLES IN LOVE

I let it go. Waves throw it back
   White bodies and twisting vines
   Wrapping on hollow trunks and slopes
   Black ocean foaming at the mouth
   Can't wait to return.

   A rose blooms, fades, dies
   and the seed wanders through
   the shade to sun, stones covering
   one by one until it can't grow
   the heart of what they knew.

   Ants dissemble a moth
   a morsel at a time
   carry it by me,
   I'm weary of seeing them.

   You break, rise up and escape
   glance away and then return
   forgetting to call
   only I don't-
   It's back again.

   13 Dec 04

HERE'S A CHILD NEVER WANTED

I'm laughing at her, that red-checked doll,
My storm I wanted to release
Like icicles hanging on the lines.

I've been hoarding the gallons of fear
For a child I didn't want
And she was redolent and wild,
Intelligent, and dam, beautiful

Mild and sweet,
And here's yours truly
Standing there hating how she strutted.
Hold me, she said.

Don't be ridiculous
I hold no one like I could hold
the smoke that circles or the clouds
That rain down in the distant in front

Of your face, Ha, a disaster, you don't see
Oh she's the city that I can't walk in
The Skyscrapers I won't go see
And the smudge of rust on the iron.

My want leaves me spoiled for a fight
There's some kind of crazy on the way
One minute, I'm sitting
The next, chewing on myself.

My mouth curses, my face is shining
As I raise my hand more
Yes, it is pouring out, more!
Yes, Anger, rage! - revenge.

13 Dec 04

NEON BRIGHT

Stab the sky again,
Watch the light bleed through
Steely bright pouring out.

She comes and goes
The buzz never stops
Lead on, lead me on.

I think it dark enough
to see the colors
evening like a sunrise

She comes and goes
like no one can.

Trying to hide
Her techno-way
She's always puzzling

In someone's business
lead on, (is this leading?)
who knows how long,

She can go before
she burns away
I can't be her angel now.

It's hard for me

to take a stand
when I want her anyway I can.

She's slipping through my hands
lead on, she's always buzzing.
How long?

19 Dec 04

TOMORROW

Tomorrow
Never showed up.
Three bands of light showed
As if to welcome where she'd start
But she didn't come.
The sky, an innocent blue,
Passed over the dirty waters
Through the city,
Waiting for the shadows to form
From humble roofs and chimneys.
I stood quietly - my soul had no arguments
Still she didn't come.
On and on, night whittles the soul
As if to say - what?
The ash is a poor rattle inside
Hardly noticeable against the din of life.

It's a sticky evening talking with Vicki
A girl I loved as a teen.
I hear the noise of the party
My Aunt Della's retired from it.
To swing and talk in front of a bright green swimming pool.

I stand in the dark hearing nothing
My insides are too noisy
And my cousins are playing games
Acting as if my Uncle lived.
"If he were here,
They said, He'd be out playing cowboy songs for everyone.
I can't hear them.

Setting beside her, I think of things to say
Between the creak of the swing now
Supporting both our weight.
She's wrinkled as the leaves falling into the pool.
She's old and his guitar sits silent.
There's no one to play it.
I haven't the heart to touch it.
She thinks it's been a good life-
(I hate conversations like that)

It means her heart has been stolen
from her as surely as the summer to autumn
steals the leaves color.
Strangers have stolen her house

And ready a place for her in a cold bed.
I wonder how many weeks she has left?
Twice a week, they promise to visit and watch her.
The coffee and the cookies are still going
When I say good night.
She pats my hand
And gives me a bullet of hope
To bite on.

12 June 05

EXPLANATIONS ON A SUMMER DAY

"How long do they live Daddy?"
She asked innocently,
Watching the fluttering wings of the butterfly
So white as angel wings
Beating the ground, helpless
Fallen from grace I think
(But I don't say)

"Only a few months" I reply.
She tries to lift it to flight
But it flutters like an old leaf
Dead and brown-
It won't fly again
Now it's just food for another
Creature, the lowest form.
(Again, I don't say)

It's sad, she tells me
Brushing away her flying gold hair
Growing up in a world
Where the discards are lost
She can't be among them,
No, not at all
The world can't be saved.
(I can't say)

12 June 05

MEMORY IN THE SNOW

And I wondered,
Standing there
Seeing how the snow
Perfectly captured
Two steps, side by side

An angel walking beside
Him? Or a second spare
Spirit, near? Who could say.
it was a pattern of close, far
Close far, a strange staggering

Nearest where the brown grass
Blades pierced the whiteness
Like a sword, frozen petals
Like iceman, staring out at
passersby. Maybe smiling

At these two, strolling, beneath
Pine tree guards, under winter's
Break of light, in spaces
Carved in themselves, in dreams
Captured right there in snow.

28 Oct 05

SAFETY

Nearly all the old words
 have decayed to mulch we
 pack around our talk-
 a Natural way to
 keep the weeds of
 real things from
 springing up. For

 an Instance
 we joke in prudent puns
 well within limits
 circular conversations
 deliberately directive to
 avoid any advancing
 truth. Her daughter's

 favorite comments
 work and I play
 along for the game
 "Math is so organized!"
 she says.
It's safe to laugh
 Here, I steer us
 Moving the rudder

 just so through this
 Placid pond-
 safe, yes, we search for

careful waters where our boat
won't tremble and
I can stay here
For a while.

5 August 05

LAST LOOK

The look on her face

Was quiet and foggy
Stayed with me all day
Like a promise I'd made.

Now the trailer is gone
And she's reduced to
treasures we might
scatter around.

Sometimes we even talk
about them, looking away
at the tears forming
trying to hide away.

Now she lives with the
crying birds, and white
clouds gathering in the
thick air and sand.

And the roses have spread
the one we shared thorns
And pain-
This woman I didn't know.

12 July 05

LISTENING WHEN YOU'RE READY

This afternoon,
The weight of the sun
Pressed you to sleep

And all I could hear
Was the quiet sighing
Of your voice.

No, that's not entirely
True, I heard the motor
Running at a constant idle

The white of the stone
Outside covered in leaves
The rustle of your blanket,

When you're ready,
I'll listen to the ants
Treading by.

20 Nov 05

WINTER'S SLOPPINESS

The sky has molted to gray
  And the tree's clothes
  Are tossed around the room
  God, I wished she'd pickup.

  Reminding her again
  Going from room to
  Room, gathering
  Straightening as the

  Light goes out
  From the windows
  And the wind knocks on
  the windows and calls

  No need to answer,
  I know this house call
  I can sit back and
  Listen to the noise.

2 Dec 05

IMAGINING RED

In the room, her pictures sit.
Black and whites, colors and smiles
stained and unstained tops of trees
and fluttering like a cotton sash
she wore that time.

Happy? Maybe busy is a better term,
too busy to fold her wings like a cloth
and settle at the amber sun, or
drop time to see direction, no time,
no time for that.

She carried herself and others.
An old shape for this room,
a sleeping child, spread out and
missing the excitement. She carried
all these things upstairs.

31 Dec 05

What is beautiful
but this island?

Short on letters
this fourth week,

I'm sitting watching
the dragon's fire
from the end of the ramp.

You're waking for work
incredible gold waves
are breaking on the beach.

Who's more stubborn
who's more alone?

29 Jan 06

IN AN ILLUSTRATOR'S APARTMENT, 1986

In her apartment,
the colors are laid out
like waves of the sun
coming through that
single window.

The cats play games at 0ne O'clock
room to room,
a rough catch-me-if-you-can
over half finished paintings propped
on a worn gray couch.

Kitchen fruit
is arranged by color
ready to be painted
among the unpaid bills
postings of upcoming shows,

Mother's recipe
for homemade pie
scent the counter and overdue
college texts with guarantees for payment.

Underfoot,
sounds of others arguments
late into the night
while you paint,
scrape
and paint again.

Canvas straightened
boxed, framed and
changed, preserved with
chemical atoms.

Patti needs umber
to finish that one.
The last tubes
are twisted snails
on the living room table.

7 march 06

CHANGING THE VOCABULARY

Even as the day begins
the very nouns modify.

A neurotic arrangement
in neuter grammar
designating neither words
or people.

What gender brings,
any new nexus breaks.

Nobility establishes
false causes, with their
nimbus shining.

A panacea of emotion
what does this bring?
Palmistry of thought.

27 Jan 05

I've turned to old writings
In the damp of November's
Cold, for I longed for the
Fire.

The key to every man is
A thought of half an angel
To spend his love with,
Suffer his heart.

What a delicacy of her soul,
To take a Portion and enjoy
Each sweet nibble,
Her lantern in the dark.

CARVINGS

A few days ago,
I was ready to press
With my sharpened knife
And carve love and hate

From the fixed feelings -
A scale you might understand.

This block of heart
A shape you might find -
A trinket size to
Display openly.

I'd use a set of knives
Carefully sized for the task.

But if I'm wrong
The cutting would only express
Hurt and scar the soft fibers-
I'm sure you'd turn away.

23 Nov 05

WIND KISSES THE WINDOW

A few days ago,
I was ready to press
With my sharpened knife
And carve love and hate

From the fixed feelings -
A scale you might understand.

This block of heart
A shape you might find -
A trinket size to
Display openly.

I'd use a set of knives
Carefully sized for the task.

But if I'm wrong
The cutting would only express
Hurt and scar the soft fibers-
I'm sure you'd turn away.

23 Nov 05

SPRING COLOR

In the spring, the great tulips
Rise up denouncing the winter
waving to me to wake up
Drink in the rain.

But now the rain is snow
drifting down in strange white
Dandruff, cursing and laughing
At the tulips voice.

This is tulips:
Brightness and alive
Dancing for the bees
Las Vegas sweet spot

Inside she feels larger
Than other flowers
It's a truism that some are
Wanted more than others!

She sometime dreams that she
Towers over the others calling out
Make me master all bees and bow
at my tasty petals.

But she doesn't cling to the past
she waits her turn, the bud will
grow, given regard for the rules
Mirrors of last spring.

She believes she's the flower
with no peer,
A sit alone place, quiet cave
for the insects to see her.

She knows to relax
No envy or jealousy knows her
guiding her hand, pressing her core
She's learned to relax.

10 April 05

SENSE OF LOSS

In this room, no one enters
The bed is perfectly made
And the pattern on the wall
Hers, cast by sunlight
On that wall -

Her last breaths
When the doctors gave in to
Shadow of a painting
Mother was finishing
Last strokes, last heartbeat.

A women I love has words in her
Hand and as her habit she
Tosses them loosely
Trying them out for sound
Click and tap like dice.

Even the ocean tries one
Thing against the sand then
Recedes and tries again
These dice don't add to score
Everyone isn't willing to count.

The kindest thing would be to
Pull the blinds, unmake the bed
And nest the details inside
Carve these back and forgive
All the years the waves washed.

6 Jan 05

THE THIRD THING

After almost two decades
  There's mystery in your eyes
  Each night,

  Still turning away at hard
  Questions,
  Still looking distant.

  In the morning, it that look
  That sends me to the kitchen
  Fixing your favorite

  Bringing it to your side
  Maybe promises later
  If time allows...

  In the day, it's your phone
  Call that breaks me from the
  Work's web choking me.

  I'm counting minutes
  Until I'm home,
 gazing into tour eyes won't happen

  You're too practical for that
  The fireplace will remain off
  Too much gas wasted.

Candles will remain unlit
Too much time, dangerous
Dangerous love - what we need

To Frolic in the night
No longer a couple
But two in one.

The slippery slope of our
First few years
Was quick-

It's the last two years
Dried in heat

A pond with a limited
Size, a vessel with cracked
Sides.

Often we'd talk of obsessive
Absorption in a nested place
No boundaries except intensity.

But for now it's ping-pong
Conversations on the bills
What she's reading.

Good theme, good ending
She tells me.
An afternoon of opportunity

Spent on other things
Not keeping score-
That wouldn't be fair.

Of course the marriage
Is made up of three things
I've forgotten the third.

1 Nov 04

LONG DIVISION

Dreams make loud
additions. I repeat
How important to know
These facts. My daughter
Shakes her head, yes.

Four eyes facing
And divided among
The rules and thoughts
When two are added
We give in as a fractions

And decimals break
Down the rules.
I'm transparent to them
And I hear your warning.
We can't do it.

Atrophy following the
Division. Disintegration-
Forget the tools of the trade
And use your head-
Score one more for pain.

21 Dec 04

TENDRILS

You are the grave's daughter
Poison writ tangled pain
cast like leaves over the porch.

When I ascend the steps into your home
I'm smothered by that pollen
soaking me and cutting me.

In dreams I walked those wood floors
looked out crazed panes
somehow they existed.

And I could breathe in that place again.
Within such time as terrible moments lived
A delirium of sleep.

A LITTLE FIRE

There's a space
Large enough for
Yourself-
A glass filled with
Sleep, growth and wisdom.

Drink and flood yourself
with this small drink
Until you're bright
Scorched bright
That I can see.

Your eye is a pearl
A beautiful thing
Receding from the distance
A trick- engaged but not-
Blank to white.

29 Nov 04

RARE EARTHS

Living or the Dead
Eventually they wash up
On your memory beach

And you must identify them
writings, papers, old test scores
report cards
Pictures.

Some of them drawn
on stony ground
With a granite name
in anger or washing sea

Who would care,
if treachery carved their name
Into its belt,
Or just took their blue eyes.

Maybe it's the mind
staring at your face
And sees you're
Shining, defeated like them.

9 October 2004

WHEN TIME TO LEAVE

Trapped in a dark, wood house
At 8, it was a prison
The Warden, with heavy hand
gave daily bruises and words.

Words were the worst part,
No one saw the damage
As I hung on the bars
And screamed out.

When the sentence was over
I left quickly without looking back,
The Warden waving like a friend
My hand was too heavy.

24 Sept 04.

RESTORATION

Everyone knew the house
Wouldn't sell
I saw their eyes turn
Away at the creaking floor
Peeling kitchen walls,

It's tiny room left
Empty after the
boy left it's banks
Left his mark high
Above the scared post.

It was left untouched
like gray river sludge
swept through the garage
my hands pink and sore
trying clean it.

Faces of relatives
Left stacked with spider
Guardians, nasty black
Toxic, venomous
Leaving their mark.

I painted squares of mild rose
On the roses, soft blue in bedroom
Trying to cover the screams
And penciled notes

A mark of growth.

I'll never know. What one part
Could match the calm beneath
The river-
A house that sold
Owners bent on restoration.

12 Nov 04

HAIKU

Cold Forest
A north wind presses
The chimney smoke.

From all directions
The lake is finally clothed
Wind brings colored leaves

A lake's blanket;
the wind brings colored leaves
from all directions

A number of geese
Produce a noisy wake
Turtles rest in sun.

CASTING STARS

My daughter has plastic
glow-in-the dark stars
glued to her ceiling.

She's named each one,
telling me:

that's one is Brian
and that one dog -

See, it's further away
because it's mean.

For seven days,
She cast them in place
and called it good.

Her own universe
without planets
wasting time revolving

without other bothersome
life to worry with.

23 Jan 06

RESOLUTIONS

In a week,
We'll be talking about resolutions.
Maybe even the things we wouldn't
say other times.
Weight can be a safe
or unsafe subject.
Writing letters,
Less time on computer,

More time on important chores.
Name them?

No time for that.
And even when you're up for it,

It's swallowed by a cool movie
or just a mess of fever
and strange passivity.

Clarity is covered in shadows
and a rose to bloom later.

One story might begin,
He did these things.

Oh, never mind,
the plow's in the barn
The earth is untouched.

ON BEING THIRTEEN

The idea excited me like the first
Smell of summer after the last school day.
First teen year would be fun,
Dad tried to tell me
Using the most bland words.

My expression must have told on me,
I tried to look interested-
But my face couldn't lie.
Thirteen would be the first views
Of my life, like getting new eyes:

The way the frost hung on the trees
And her moist lips looked as I wondered
How it would be, just to have her say
My name. (Am I supposed to know now?)
At this uncultured, unseasoned stage.

Now I'm watching at the window
As the late afternoon light.
This side of the house cooling,
My bicycle resting against the mesquite tree
I'd never ride the same.

30 Jan 05

COUNTING THEIR DRESSES

He stood by the pavement
Counting each car passing
Until the sunflowers smiled at him.

He fell in to them.
They flirted with their yellow dresses
Flashing him in the sun

Twisted their bodies
In a floor show of
Wind and sun's light.

After that, he couldn't
Help but be captured,
Drunk as a gravel stone

Flowers continued
Brushing their lips against him,
Even the tiny black ant waiters teased him.

But work still called,
The papers in his case yelling
Pointing at their watches, it's time.

Dave

ZERO

These days as the wind blows
I lay my head down and hear
My house strains against the
wind's shoulder. I'm wrapped

In night's skin,
She presses against me.
cold as it hugs me. I'm
Sleeping alone, starving

In the love's zero degrees
replaying furious dreams
A closet full of skeletons
Grinning at the cost.

24 August 05

OIL PAINTING

I like to lay you down,
In even paper traces without
A pause, without a margin to
tackle, like an endless autumn
day to enjoy, a surface of oil
I can run my fingers in-

That's it, a soft, warm soothing oil
Traced on your skin, I can write
Without control, without time
No responsible sketches-
We should try now, touch the
Creases and bring the breath

back to you. Hold the pen lightly
And touch the careful spots gliding
Over my letters, let me write each
One in capitals, spelling the secrets
We won't write anywhere else- they're
Written in fragrance, soft friction

And ways I can't overcome, like final words
And currents ruffling your quiet leaves-
Guess the messages I write, the shape of
Each letter, your mouth is open in
Pronouncing each one, You're eyes shut
Naming the words I'm saying.

4 September 05

MOM'S WALLS MAKE NO SOUND

At Mom's house, the wood floors
Haven't seen a broom-
The dust floats in cotton puffs
Around the corners, as her
Doors open and close slowly.

All the dreams live in soiled boxes
Under her bed, closed off to eyes,
Photos I've never seen - hiding
In collapsing paper and yellowing sheets
Of crumpled plastic.

Breakfast is dark coffee that fills
the house with it's burnt odor, tempered by cream
Dad pours a few drips at a time.
She'd rather would have been making
Sandwiches and lunches but She didn't make one - now
her hands are cracked

At dusk she visits the yard remembering
A tended garden and the bounty from it
But never the details of who did it
(No never that.)
She won't remember.

Beneath her sleep, the stars never bloomed
stars that called me desperately
how many cold stars
In her embrace - How many?
I can't count.

Open mom's cabinets and see the same
Cracked dishes and cups there,
Never replace, never.
Each drawer is filled with sharp knives
and a warning - don't touch them.

My mom weaves a nest of sleep
A forgotten nest there
But I'm not able to incubate my sleep
Because she shakes the air
And tells me to wake quickly.

The hypothesis: I'm tense and you aren't.
We are lines that always cross
Therefore we cannot be parallel
And I can't find the angle.
The Proof: If we are two arcs
Cutting across the page,
Somewhere we must meet and
Our lines agree? At least for now.
If the lines are bisected by a third
(In my case, tension)
Find the solutions when the strain
Forces are greatest-
You can find it.
So, we must be congruent-
The third line crossing the same point,
Equal angles at least to the third.
But no, this theory fails too.
And so, we're left measuring angles
Computing sums and waiting
to be parallel.

19 Feb 05

DIFFERENCES

There is a difference
Between solitude
And loneliness
A story told over a
Single river that
Dries out to clay

Or a strong green pine
That lifts itself
Above the wet earth
Over the mist and
Heat, for the birds to
Find and roost in.

I can carry both
Through the house
Like a sleeping child
But only one will
Remember the story
The next day.

14 July 05

LANDSCAPE

No arranged trees there,
No split-barked sycamore
Scattered about,
Staving off insects,

No flare of flowers,
Carefully bunched together
Behind protected plastic fences
On a steep hill.

No branch of Japanese Maple
Breaking out in confetti spring
To the silhouettes of crows
against the sky,

An unencumbered blue
Scrubbed to emptiness
By the long wind through
The hair unnumbered on our heads.

It's all higher than ourselves
No shadow veil of perfection
Or human hand on the
Barest earth's breast.

17 April 05

COLOR OF HER LAUGH

Even in the faintest light
It blooms, spreading it
Thought, it's taste.

Why it seems bitter, I
Want to ask: Do you know
How this feels to see
That color and it's inky
Black texture spreading
Across my heavy winter.

Her whisper calls across
Icy time in the snow
Reflects spiky words.

Fade and draw back
Wait for the close-up and
Scene to take me in
For the color, the changing
The plotting of the next
Laugh.

4 October 2005

UNTITLED

I'm not a gatherer of sea treasures
but for the man with basket
the clank of shells
weaves his desires.

March 5, 2006

HAIKU

In the sun's petals,
Spring has begun to pass
I wasn't finished with sorrows.

HANDS

The boy only wanted to show
His mother something new
After all her roses had bloomed
Looking at him as he came
She decided her roses were gone.

All she could see is where the thorns
Pierced, buried deep inside,
And the tears that he cried,
Though she wouldn't tend his wounds.
But he was showing his love.

Even when the scars showed themselves
Her lap she wouldn't share,
But he knew it was love.
It had to be Buried,
That's how he hurt his hand.

The boy's moved out on his own
Uncle Sam called him along
with luck, he moved far away
It wasn't long that overseas
Before, he took his hands.

Each night wanting to share
roses he saw, past victory
glory, sorrows
But the roses had bloomed,
And the thorns gone away.

Well, years have past
And he was sure he understood
Letters and news before they came
He was showing his love
And that's how he hurt his hand.

27 Dec 04

BENT

It's a quiet rebellion
Bent over and formed in a silent C.
Unsteady, softly walking with help
On the grey cobble stones.
His aged, white hair wife
Holding him.

His white pony tail streaming down
A forgotten display of strength
A forgotten show to others-
He's beyond society and rules
Rules about life
He thought he cheated.

5 June 05

BEYOND

I listen for the movement
Return of the evening
The sky dressed in night clothes
A hushed gray, over starlight

It's the way we do business
Sublimation and cold duties the
Way blame takes the arrow, the
Way the owls finds the mouse.

Whole people disappear while she
Hunts in the field
Slow dancing with moonlight
Beyond our hearing.

1 Jan 05

CARD GAME

I believe that life
Cheated you at cards-
Always showing an
Ace when you thought
You'd won.
So, the pain plays
Out of every syllable
Even when you thought
We weren't watching.
Anger and depression
Were busy enemies
Steeling any Hope
Or joy
Right out of your mouth.
Music has to be
Formal and slow
Causing that long face
To permanently stay
In your clenched fists.

10 July 05

BREAKING THINGS

You've broken so many things
I don't bother keeping them.

I found the place
where I can throw

the shells,
ocean
music
notes
wood

away.

29 Jan 06

BREAKING SILENCE

We walked along the bleached beach homes
Where the edge of the surf splashed
Where the sun was a red dot,

All the evening, we watched the line
Change from distant to a few feet away
Toward the edge of the walk.

Back and forth talk was flattened
By the water's voice.
Intimacy is killed yelling over the wind.

On this last day,
I wondered when the surf would settle
And the crabs would stop scuttling around.

24 Nov 05

BREEZE

So many dead afternoons
Spent taling about weather.

The breeze suggests a thin
Blue smoke curling
Pine's perfume twists from

Your chimney, the
Damage is done
Even slight-
(How would I know?)

You could be showing
Sail , masts of new
Leaves liter the air.
Limbs snapping,

Widespread destruction,
Standing in debris
Let loose and fly.

9 Jan 05

CARRIER

My mother was a carrier
And maybe her father before
Him, I don't know.
But I've seen her buckets
Filled with all the
Toxic liquids

She's spilled out all
My life.
(I can only speak of this)

Three parts of Anger
Hate mixed
Rejection's acid-
All the right substances
Causing the most
Damage in its splashes,

Spills I've walked through
And to my own buckets
(What's in them?)

28 July 05

CLOCK STOP

Each time I step
Into my backyard,
It seems different.

Yes, yes, the roses are there
And that peach tree
Looking more sickly each day

But it's all different.
The clock in the bedroom
Has been stopped for weeks.

It's always late now to read
Rest or relax.
(So, I'm told)

And I'm spending too much time
Worried about being remembered
Casting stones into the future.

25 Jan 05

CLOTHING

No matter how you clothe the young
Foolishness, malice and hate
Can't be covered.

No matter how you clothe the wind
Rain, snow and hail
Still come in the night.

19 Feb 05

COLD

January is a childless skyline
Branches without leaves,
Unsettled, an earth without
A stitch of clothing.
An ear waiting for snow,
Uncertain what direction
We're going now.

I hear crying in the fierce
Wind, pieces of snow dancing
In the wild rhythm while they
Wander, wander and stare
Back in the light of the open
Door, the footsteps perishing
Outside's sudden decoration.

13 Jan 05

UNTITLED

This was vacation,
This was resting
hearing the same
clank and tones
amid the chores,
spelled out in stones-
that sandstone
reminds me to take
the ground, grain by grain
and clean it out.
That broken Aspen
heap reminds me
to tidy my thoughts
back to one direction.

The coffee stains
on the table flow
one way, on the silver sink,
grease slips, slides on the dishes.

These simple needs don't change.

The world must turn the same,
Same angle with our
alabaster buddy
trailing behind at a
respectable distance

growing dim then bright
dim, then bright
shaking the sea into compliance.

See, it's high then
low and no matter where your place
it won't change.

20 Jan 06

Today I am the color of the morning
Anticipating skies, for the cool
Autumn that waits, arrives on
Bright leafy flags. Yes, to
Walk its cottonwood fields, A
Yellow and ochre parade along
Our chocolate river now ebbing
Along, leaving deep banks.
Autumn slows everything.

WHERE DEPRESSION'S WATERS DEEP

Where waters are deep
The waves wash and wash
Yet never cleanse
Even the shallow parts

Not one grain of sand
Moves on and on
Or sees the warmth
Of the suns eyes.

Only a constant evening
Paleness, leaked in a little
At time, a room of dark
With atmospheres of deepness.

A breath that goes in short
Puffs and returns in shadows
When the next one comes
It's not welcome to arrive

But only questioned for the solace
It brings for the moment
Complete chronicles revisited
Inside and out.

My father was a messenger
A bringer of reality
Layered out into life,
My mother, a bring of the deep

A place where the well rings
And rings but never brings
Freshness, not one drop
That would soothe.

My Grandfather toiled in
Deepness and brought life
To visitors only
Never to family

Woe to the family
Who sat at his table-
Not even the honey was sweet
Or the bread he cut.

29 May 05

DELTA

What a difference between us
You would use the afternoon
Reminding me of duty's spikes
Pulling us into a deep lake

I would spend the afternoon
walking from sycamore to
Pine, taking in the shade
Like a slow breath

Nothing could diminish
My heart on this
This blue sky euphoria
In the highest degree.

You don't seem to mind
That we disagree
On what safe and quiet is
And there's a difference.

15 July 05

DESERT SOUNDS

Keeping time,
The soft, deep rhyme
Across the valley
In A flat, the train wail sounds
A lament across the desert.

4 Jan 05

A LITTLE DESERT NIGHT

There's a pattern of loose leaves
Woven into the corner
Where my white glittering rocks were.

In strange terms
Mums shout their last few colors,
And The design changes from blue to gray,

Maybe the earth could run backwards
And the story could be retold
From somewhere color sunsets are stored.

By lamplight, the earth is jaundice
Feeling the sudden cold faintly coming
Woven into the night's fine fabric.

3 Nov 05

DIFFERENCES

There is a difference
Between solitude
And loneliness-
A story told over a
Single river that
Dries out to clay

Or a strong green pine
That lifts itself
Above the wet earth
Over the mist and
Heat, for the birds to
Find and roost in.

I can carry both
Through the house
Like a sleeping child
But only one will
Remember the story
The next day.

14 July 05

DOUBLE FOOL

I am a double fool
For loving and saying
Out loud my commitment
In poetry.

For in this world
Wise men deny the
Need to lock into
Any vow.

Less the narrow way
Crooked lanes would
Dam the fierceness
Tame it.

So what have I done?
Voice his art, pain
And sing upon the pages
Grief.

ALL THAT REMAINS

All that remains is the smoldering coals
Those embers have fully burned
And the smoke curls upward in slow dances.

Perhaps now, I can touch this fire
I can reach in and dare to see the parts
brush the thin dust layer.

There it is, the charred
Heart I thought wouldn't survive
After the fire has burned down.

2 May 05

EASY

I could walk out
And fall in love with the stars
Pouring out like a thousand candles
All praying for the soul that got away.

Covering the soft table of the earth
Across the tabernacle and the wisp
Of pine smoke incense that wraps
The house tops in their arms.

I could fall for the soft leaf mosaic
The fall seamstress spread everywhere
A prayer rug, I should spend time on
Counting the stones like beads.

This is the best kind,
Not expecting, not late or delayed
Held back or jealous
Just loving and going on.

19 Nov 05

EXILE

I am a dark cloud
Who cannot call home, a churning
Tide of silty gray ocean
You can't look into and
Feel safe enough to enter

A dangerous reef
To avoid, forsaken shore
Without a name, place
Where the fear of breaking
Waters courses over you.

Drowning out my voice with
A splash and thought. Amid
Drunken waters, I lie here
Growing colder, wondering if the
Stars would even reflect in me.

1 August 05
Inspired by Michelle Gould Poem

FACES WE MAKE

"Did you see that face?" She asked
Pointing back with her thumb. It was
Cold and forced as the tide, reluctant
To kiss the beach,

Maybe because she's tired,
Or this job isn't a fun.
Maybe it's pain,

Running down her face and
Stopping at her mouth,
Breaking out in twisted turns.

At the bottom of the sea,
The light doesn't reach
And the tide doesn't see

To refresh and bring life
Again, against the strange
Weather at the surface.

20 Nov 05

FIGURES

I'm a mirror dream.
A second calculation
resulting in null and
infinity at the same
instant.

I'm clumsy and fitted
to the same tired cloth.
A mountain refusing to
wear down with the
sepia sky line.

Maybe you'd share
everything about me.
A shared hollow history-
whether I like it or not, it
can't be a secret.

When I recollect the dream
It's an empty set,
soundless entries,
An unsent letter.

15 Dec 05

FIRST THINGS

The first thing I must do is cry
But the sky was completely clear
Bent into the shape of the wind
Over flapping tent,
Caught together with the gulls
Turning like strange sailing
Beasts-
Like welcoming guardians
To welcome Uncle home, But I
Didn't. I was Like the dry wood
Casket, standing on it's stern
Looking at the lacy insides saying
Control, control the wood
Understood?
No-
Everyone was raining, wring the
Sponge: Our generations
But I was too far to justify
Too far to see the bones raised
To see the last ticking of the
Clock, and say goodbye.

2 August 05

FOR SOME REASON

I can walk in the
Deep fields
Outside my house
Sharpening my senses

The sixth one is water-

And it flowed over
What you didn't say.
The grey waters of
Your eyes swimming.

I could see the secret-

Without a sign or sound
Hanging on the edge of
A wide river
Spring was miles away

When the ice broke.

3 July 05

HORIZONS

Each western painting have
Converging lines that spell a
Point where reality fades to guesses
And Even the simple break of
Color can't decide the outcome.

Funny, Japanese painting lack
Convergence. Maybe because they
Can't see the changes or where
Any points fade or maybe it's because
They don't concern themselves with

Outside the lines and focus on
The shallow, translucent tones and
Barren cherry limbs hanging over
Waters, a single koi circling
Reality to a fixed point.

4 September 05

LOVE TURNED INSIDE OUT

When love is skinned
And it's coat turned
inside out,

A reeking stench
fills the room.
a scouring coarseness

pressing and tearing
every flesh with its
smile.

Who can wear it?
Who can stand its heavy
Pressing weight.

12 Dec 05

INVITATIONS

At the bookstore,
Vanilla riches are
Pouring out from coffees

Sipped between the
Turns of pages and
Muttered conversations
(As crickets)

Silent as I come in
Suddenly grim at
My approach

Suddenly cut off
Like his charred hair
On his left side,

Her Face,
Powder white
Styles I don't understand.

My desired book is
Already gone so I
View the world again as

I retreat along the
Same path
Past the open

Mouths and
Silence, the
Borders of

Flowing sentences
Stopped in mid-gap.
Viewed from

outside its
Surreal to
Stall history like this.

27 July 05

KEEPERS

After the hospital and
Services over his coffin
Some years later, the
Powdery white photos

Water damaged and
Faded come to visit
Finding all the
Trips we wish we'd

Made over that
Wooden, creaking bridge
Where the wild Lupine
Bloomed near the road

Remember where we'd stopped?
Photos of us when we were
Babies and you were beat at
Chess. Don't forget your

Dreams and anger's storm
You brewed it to bitterness,
Put a placeholder and
Decide to keep it.

2 Sept 05
Inspired by Herman Asarnow Poem.

KINGDOMS

Thus, I divided our yard,
Giving at least part of
The grass a decent life
Honey suckle fragrance is

Free to drift over it
Not constrained by
Borders but watered
Like a light silver crown
it bows it's

Head to put on and
Smiles, calling
Gentile subjects, I'm
Glad to call this kingdom
My own, to

Cast the light of my reign
Over you and
Fill your courts with
Gladness and good

Tidings until
Wood recapture our land
And return it to
Heathen hands, our

River has crossed
Itself again, leaving her
Rich banks and returning
Chaos. I divided and

It will be undivided
When my dirty hands
Can turn its soil
No longer.

7 August 05

LULLABY

Slipping under the silver waves of sleep
Turn your mind in the fertile soil of dreams.
Certainly the joy of a child's laughter
Caught in play, her blond hair soaring
A melody you love to hear again and again.

How wisdom reflected in the quiet pond
Of truth, your life a simple reed
Appearing for a moment,
What insight you gained, sugar clouds
in an azure sky, floating by.

Sleep is a ship you sail on and on
And each grey wave sinks down further
All is fresh and free
In this ocean for a time,
For this journey.

7 June 05

NEARLY SLEEPING

My mind drifts off to a silent pond
Interrupted by a distant page turn
Your sigh at a chapter's end.

Surely you see me,
Leaning on sleep's door
Eyes flickering on and off.

But you're locked to the beat,
Scratch of your fingers on a margin
My soul on the margin of rest.

4 Feb 05

NEARLY WINTER

It's cold outside
Dropped in blue skies
It should be snowing
We would be driving
Slowly, sloshing through
Dirty, icy puddles
At 8:00 a.m., impatience
Would pour out everywhere
At the speed of anger.

5 Oct 05

UNTITLED

When I'm alone in the dark I
There's no space or time
Only intensity and tame things
Having no immensity. All

Is distant and shadows of
Sea sounds waving the trees
Like giant paintbrushes painting
Our sky with depth. All night I hear

Colors going on, the brush cleaned
Then, stroking again, so soft, in
Sienna shades, wondering what the
Canvas will show by morning.

Dave

NUMBER FUN

Eight was late
And laid to rest
Found infinite
Has slept beside it.

Six as a numb and
Caught the sum
As it stayed in line to
Catch.

Four was a door
Or maybe a ship that
Sails away into the
Night.

Two and five were confused
Written one way, I can't
Tell who they are. Six and
Nine did the same game.

Three went bottom up
And Scared away the group,
Seven was a lazy L
Shepherding the Troup.

28 August 05

QUESTIONS TO ASK

Is my soul solid
An iron framework
I've poured my heart into.

Safe? from the world
And it's rancor?
The howl of the wind?

Or is it tender, breakable
Like the brittle limbs
Where life has leaked away.

Surely not a moth
Who's silvery magic wipes away
Leaving the creature flightless.

And what shape does it take
An iceberg?
I can only see one tenth.

A flittering hummingbird
Buzzing between trumpet flowers
On a time schedule she can't break?

10 April 05

About the Author

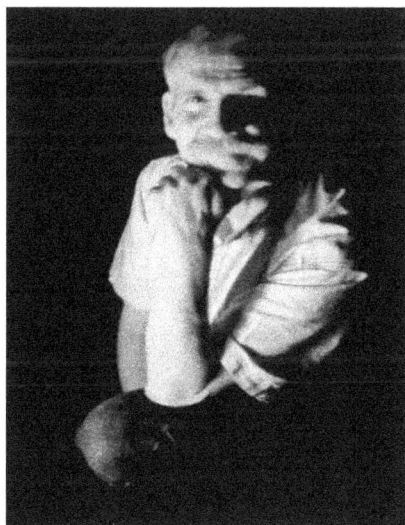

David Barber has been a writer of poetry for almost thirty years. He is the writer of two other books of poetry "Life in a Minor Key" and "Painting with Fingers" that were inspired by his experience with his childhood and being a parent. His work has appeared in a number of anthologies and magazines including Southeast Magazine and Beach Town Press. Dave was born in south Texas and lives in the beautiful mountains of Albuquerque New Mexico.

ALL THINGS THAT MATTER PRESS ™

FOR MORE INFORMATION ON TITLES AVAILABLE FROM
ALL THINGS THAT MATTER PRESS, GO TO
http://allthingsthatmatterpress.com
or contact us at
allthingsthatmatterpress@gmail.com

www.ingramcontent.com/pod-product-compliance
Lightning Source LLC
Chambersburg PA
CBHW032017090426
42741CB00006B/638